vegetarian

igloo

igloo

Published by Igloo Books Ltd
Cottage Farm
Sywell
NN6 0BJ
www.igloo-books.com

10 9 8 7 6 5 4 3 2

ISBN: 978 1 84817 636 2

Project Managed by R&R Publications Marketing Pty Ltd

Food Photography: R&R Photostudio (www.rrphotostudio.com.au)
Recipe Development: R&R Test Kitchen

Front cover photograph © Stockfood/Eising

Printed and manufactured in India

contents

introduction   4

soups and starters   8

side dishes   30

main courses   50

salads   70

potatoes   92

index   110

introduction

Vegetarian eating is a healthy alternative for today's lifestyle. Meals without meat or poultry are attractive, tasty and satisfying – as well as being good for you. The recipes in this book provide delectable dishes which can be combined or enjoyed as a hearty meal on their own. Influenced by cuisines from around the world, there are easy-to-prepare dishes which have the wonderful texture and flavour of fresh vegetables, raw and cooked.

From an Asian-influenced soup to scrumptious desserts, this selection of satisfying and delicious recipes will enable you to prepare natural healthy food for every appetite and occasion, from a quick snack to a three-course dinner party.

VEGETABLE KNOW-HOW

To make the most of your garden-fresh vegetables, we've put together these essential step-by-step preparation and cooking tips.

READY

Easy preparation and cooking depends on having a few good basic pieces of equipment. To make life easier, it's worth investing in a large chopping board, a small sharp vegetable or paring knife, several larger sharp knives for cutting and chopping, a grater, a vegetable peeler and a colander or large sieve. Remember to keep your knives sharp: either learn to sharpen them yourself or take them to a knife sharpener regularly. Sharp knives make preparation a breeze.

SET

Wash vegetables before preparing, but do not soak. Soaking tends to draw out the valuable water-soluble vitamins and you end up with vegetables with a lower nutrient content. If you do find it necessary to soak very dirty vegetables to remove grime and creepy-crawlies, keep the soaking time to a minimum.

- Vegetables left whole with their skins on have a higher nutrient and fibre content than those that are finely chopped and peeled. Many of the precious vitamins and minerals in vegetables are stored just under the skin, so only peel vegetables if necessary.

- For maximum nutritional value, prepare vegetables just before cooking and serve them as soon as they're cooked.

- The smaller the portion, the quicker the cooking time. For example, grated carrot will cook more quickly than carrot cut into slices.

GO

- To cube, cut into about 1cm pieces.

- To dice, cut into 5mm pieces.

- To grind, cut into 2.5mm pieces.

- To grate, use either a hand grater or a food processor with a grating attachment.

- To slice, cut from very thin to thick. You can also slice into rings. Another way to slice is to cut diagonally. This is a good way to prepare vegetables such as carrots, celery and courgette for stir-frying.

REMEMBER THE THREE M'S

- Minimum water

- Minimum cooking

- Minimum cutting

GOOD FOR YOU

Health authorities recommend that we eat five servings of fruit and vegetables daily, at least one of which should be raw. The old adage of a white, a yellow and a green may be rarely taught these days, but it's a good reminder that brightly coloured vegetables are usually the best source of vitamins.

PANTRY PLANNING

Try the following tips for no-fuss pantry planning.

- If you store herbs and spices in alphabetical order, they are easily located and you can see when they need replacing.

- Growing a few herbs of your own such as basil, coriander, rosemary, mint, chives and parsley means you always have these on hand. Fresh herbs are often the secret to delicate flavours in meals.

- Place all staples, such as sugar and flour together. Store sauces and condiments according to your favourite cuisines; just a glance in the cupboard will give you great ideas.

- Keep a good selection of frozen vegetables. Peas, beans, spinach and corn are great standbys and take only minutes to cook in the microwave.

- Keep a variety of breads and rolls in the freezer and defrost in the microwave for delicious instant sandwiches.

- Cooked pasta and rice freeze well; reheat in minutes in the microwave and save time on busy nights.

- Evaporated milk, also available in low-fat, is a terrific standby when there is no fresh cream. It can be used for sauces and quiches and it whips well when chilled. Store a few cans in the pantry for emergencies.

Left to right: cubed, diced, grinded, grated, sliced

FIBRE IN VEGETABLES

VEGETABLE	SERVE	FIBRE(G)*
Asparagus, boiled	6–8 spears(55g)	1.4
Beans, green, raw	½ cup (6g)	1.2
Bean sprouts	2 tablespoons (10g)	0.3
Beetroot, canned	2 slices (20g)	0.6
Broccoli, boiled	⅔ cup (100g)	3.9
Cabbage, white, boiled	½ cup (6g)	1.0
Courgette, boiled	1 medium (110g)	1.5
Pepper, green, raw	¼ cup (40g)	0.5
Carrot, peeled, boiled	1 carrot (100g)	2.9
Cauliflower, boiled	⅔ cup (100g)	2.0
Celery, raw	1 stalk (100g)	0.8
Chilli, raw	2 chillies (6g)	0.6
Corn	½ cup kernels (75g)	3.5
Cucumber, peeled, raw	4–5 slices (20g)	0.1
Aubergine, baked	½ small (75g)	2.7

VEGETABLE	SERVE	FIBRE(G)*
Garlic, raw	2 cloves (10g)	1.7
Leek, boiled	1 leek (6g)	1.4
Lettuce, raw	2 leaves (20g)	0.1
Mushrooms, fried	4–6 mushrooms (75g)	1.4
Olives	3 green (20g)	0.8
Onion, peeled, fried	1 onion (80g)	2.2
Parsley	2 sprigs (2g)	0.1
Peas, green, boiled	⅓ cup (40g)	1.0
Potato, peeled, roasted	1 medium (120g)	2.4
Potato, unpeeled, boiled	1 medium (120g)	3.0
Pumpkin, peeled, boiled	½ cup (80g)	2.4
Radish, red, raw	2 radishes (10g)	0.1
Chard, boiled	3 stalks (100g)	2.1
Tomato, raw	1 medium (130g)	2.4

*grams of dietary fibre per serve

soups and starters

Avocado Gazpacho

(see photograph opposite)

2 large ripe avocados, stoned, peeled and chopped

grated zest and juice of 1 lemon

2½ cups vegetable stock

2 large tomatoes

1 cucumber, chopped

1 green and 1 red pepper, deseeded and chopped

1 clove garlic, crushed

salt and black pepper

4 tablespoons freshly snipped chives to garnish

1 Place the avocados, lemon zest and juice and the stock in a food processor and blend to a thin, smooth purée (or use a hand blender). Pour into a large bowl and set aside.

2 Place the tomatoes in a bowl, cover with boiling water and leave for 30 seconds. Remove from the bowl, peel off the skins, then deseed and chop the flesh. Reserve a little chopped tomato and cucumber to garnish. Place the rest of the tomatoes and cucumber in the food processor with the peppers, garlic and seasoning, then blend to a purée. Alternatively, use a hand blender.

3 Add the tomato mixture to the avocado purée, mixing thoroughly. Cover and refrigerate for 1 hour, then serve garnished with chives and the reserved tomato and cucumber.

Serves 4

Note: On a balmy summer evening, what better start to a meal than this iced gazpacho with its extra avocado? Serve with crusty bread to mop up the last delicious drop!

Bruschetta and Crostini

(see photograph page 8)

BRUSCHETTA

garlic bread

thick slices of bread

1 clove garlic

olive oil

CROSTINI

small rounds or squares of bread

olive oil or melted butter

BRUSCHETTA

1 Grill bread slices on both sides. Crush and peel garlic. Rub over the bread. Drizzle over olive oil. Use as wished.

CROSTINI

1 Brush bread with olive oil or melted butter. Grill until lightly toasted or bake at 190°C for 5 minutes.

Serves 4

Note: Suit yourself on what you make. Both are delicious and make a useful base for all sorts of vegetables, spreads and toppings.

Tuscan Bean and Bread Soup

½ loaf ciabatta bread

3 tablespoons olive oil

3 onions, chopped

3 cloves garlic, chopped

2 x 400g canned chopped tomatoes

400g canned flageolet beans

2½ cups vegetable stock

salt and black pepper

basil leaves to garnish

1 Preheat the oven to 150°C. Cut the ciabatta into dice, then place in the oven for 10 minutes to dry out.

2 Heat the oil in a large saucepan, add the onions and garlic, and cook for 3–4 minutes, until soft. Add the tomatoes, beans and stock, bring to the boil, then simmer for 2 minutes.

3 Stir in the diced ciabatta, bring the soup back to the boil, then simmer for a further 5 minutes. Season, then serve garnished with basil.

Serves 4

Leek, Lime and Coconut Soup

2 tablespoons olive oil

3 leeks, thinly sliced

1 green chilli, deseeded
   and chopped

2 potatoes, diced

grated zest and juice of 2 limes,
   plus a few extra slices to garnish

salt and black pepper

2¼ cups vegetable stock

1 cup coconut milk

coriander leaves to garnish

1 Heat the oil in a large heavy-based saucepan, then add the leeks, chilli,
   potatoes, lime zest and seasoning. Cook for 2 minutes, then add the stock
   and bring to the boil. Reduce the heat and simmer for 20–25 minutes, until
   the potatoes are tender. Leave to cool slightly.

2 Transfer the soup to a food processor and blend briefly to make a chunky,
   creamy mixture, or use a hand blender. Return the soup to the pan.

3 Stir in the lime juice, then add the coconut milk and heat through, taking care
   not to let the soup boil. Serve hot or cold, garnished with slices of lime and
   the coriander.

Serves 4

*Note: The Thai flavours of lime and coconut totally transform this classic leek
and potato soup. You can enjoy it hot or cold, depending on your mood and
the weather.*

Spinach and Almond Soup

(see photograph opposite)

500g baby spinach

3½ cups vegetable stock

100g ground almonds

salt and black pepper

½ cup single cream

60g Parmesan cheese, grated,
  to garnish

1   Put the spinach into a large saucepan with the stock, reserving a few leaves to garnish. Bring to the boil, then reduce the heat and simmer for 5 minutes. Stir in the almonds and seasoning and simmer for 2 minutes. Remove from the heat and leave to cool a little.

2   Pour into a food processor and blend to a smooth purée, or use a hand blender. Add the cream, return to the pan and reheat gently – don't let the soup boil. Serve topped with the Parmesan and a sprinkling of pepper, and garnished with the reserved spinach.

Serves 4

Note: Not only do the almonds add their distinctive taste to this spinach soup, they also give it a lovely thick texture. It's delicious hot or cold – especially if you use fresh stock.

Creamy Aubergine Topping

(see photograph page 8)

1 medium aubergine

3 cloves garlic

2 tablespoons olive oil

2 tablespoons lemon juice

salt

freshly ground black pepper

bruschetta or crostini

fresh basil leaves

1   Please aubergine on a baking tray with unpeeled garlic and grill under a hot grill, turning until aubergine is black on all sides. Take care not to puncture the aubergine. Turn garlic regularly and remove from grill if the skin starts to brown. Whenaubergine is black and soft remove from oven. Leave to cool. Peel away aubergine skin, drain if necessary and mash the flesh. Peel garlic and mash flesh with eggplant. Add olive oil, lemon juice, salt and pepper to aubergine puree. Mix well. Use to top bruschetta or crostini. Garnish with torn basil leaves.

Makes 1½ cups

Roasted Pepper Topping

(see photograph page 8)

2 red peppers

1 yellow peppers

1 green peppers

1 clove garlic

1 tablespoon olive oil

1 tablespoon white vinegar

freshly ground black pepper

bruschetta or crostini

1   Cut peppers in half lengthwise. Remove seeds and stems. Place cut-side down on an oven tray and grill until the skin is blistered and brown. Wrap in foil and leave to cool. Remove skins and cut flesh into thin strips. Crush and peel garlic and chop finely. Mix pepper strips, garlic, oil, vinegar and pepper together. Use to top bruschetta or crostini.

Makes 1½ cups

Thick Minestrone with Pesto

3 tablespoons olive oil

1 onion, chopped

2 cloves garlic, chopped

1 potato, cut into 1cm cubes

2 small carrots, cut into 1cm cubes

1 large courgette, cut into 1cm cubes

¼ white cabbage, chopped

3 cups vegetable stock

2 x 400g canned chopped tomatoes

90g pasta shapes, such as
   conchiglie shells

salt and black pepper

5 tablespoons Parmesan cheese, grated

5 tablespoons pesto

1 Heat the oil in a large heavy-based saucepan, then add the onion, garlic, potato, carrots, courgette and cabbage and cook for 5–7 minutes, until slightly softened.

2 Add the stock and tomatoes and bring to the boil. Reduce the heat and simmer for 20 minutes, then add the pasta and seasoning and cook for a further 15 minutes or until the pasta is tender but still firm to the bite. Divide the soup between bowls, top each with a tablespoon of Parmesan and pesto and serve.

Serves 4

Curried Cream of Vegetable Soup

4 tablespoons groundnut or
  vegetable oil

3 tablespoons curry powder

pinch each of ground cinnamon,
  nutmeg, turmeric and ginger

3 carrots, diced

2 onions, chopped

2 cloves garlic, chopped

2 potatoes, diced

2 courgettes, diced

4 cups vegetable stock

300g canned cannellini beans, drained

300g canned red kidney beans,
  drained

⅔ cup crème fraîche

salt

2 teaspoons chopped fresh Italian
  parsley to garnish

1 Place the oil in a large heavy-based saucepan. Add the curry powder,
   cinnamon, nutmeg, turmeric and ginger and cook for 1 minute, then add the
   carrots, onions, garlic, potatoes and courgettes. Stir to coat thoroughly in the
   oil and spice mixture and cook for a further 5 minutes.

2 Add the stock and bring to the boil. Reduce the heat and simmer for
   20 minutes or until the vegetables are tender. Add the cannellini and red
   kidney beans and gently heat through. Remove from the heat and stir in the
   crème fraîche. Season to taste and serve sprinkled with the parsley.

Serves 4

*Note: A dollop of crème fraîche makes a creamy contrast to the spicy
flavour of this versatile soup. Use seasonal vegetables, and serve with warm
French bread.*

Artichokes with Sour Cream Sauce

4 large globe artichokes

salt

1¼ cups sour cream

5 spring onions, finely chopped

1 tablespoon balsamic vinegar

1 clove garlic, finely chopped

1   Cut off the artichoke stalks, so that the artichokes stand flat. Place in a large saucepan of boiling salted water and simmer, partly covered, for 40 minutes or until tender. To test if the artichokes are cooked, pull off an outside leaf – it should come away easily. Remove the artichokes from the pan and set aside for 30 minutes to cool.

2   Meanwhile, make the sauce. Mix together the sour cream, spring onions, vinegar and garlic. Pull the central cone of leaves out of each artichoke, leaving a wall of leaves around the edge, and discard. Scrape away the inedible core with a teaspoon, to leave the edible base.

3   Spoon plenty of sauce into the artichoke centre. Place the artichokes on plates and serve. Eat by plucking out a leaf and dipping it into the sauce. Use your teeth to pull away the edible fleshy part at the base of the leaf, then discard the rest.

Serves 4

Note: Serving artichokes in this classic way is simpler than you may think. And the best bit – the base of the artichoke covered with rich, creamy sauce – is saved until last.

Courgette Rounds with Pepper Purée

3 courgettes, grated

salt

4 tablespoons snipped fresh chives, plus extra to garnish

2 tablespoons chopped fresh coriander, plus extra leaves to garnish

½ teaspoon grated nutmeg

1 spring onion, finely chopped, to garnish

PURÉE

3 tablespoons olive oil

3 red peppers, cored, deseeded and chopped

salt and black pepper

1 Sprinkle the courgettes with salt, place in a colander, then set aside for 30 minutes to draw out the excess moisture. Rinse under cold running water, then squeeze dry and mix with the chives, coriander and nutmeg. Pack the mixture into 4 ramekins – it should half-fill them. Refrigerate for 1 hour, or overnight.

2 To make the purée, put the oil into a saucepan, then add the peppers and season. Cook, covered, over a low heat for 15 minutes. Leave to cool for a few minutes, then blend to a smooth purée in a food processor, or with a hand blender. Press the purée through a sieve to remove the skins.

3 To serve, turn each ramekin onto a plate, giving it a sharp shake to dislodge the courgette round, then spoon around the sauce. Garnish with the chives, spring onion and coriander.

Serves 4

Note: Courgette's subtle flavour is enhanced by the coriander, nutmeg and chives, then combined with the sweetness of the fresh red pepper purée.

Sweet Pepper Terrine with Basil Vinaigrette

(see photograph opposite)

butter for greasing

2 red and 2 yellow peppers, halved
  and deseeded

4 tablespoons olive oil

1 red chilli, deseeded and thinly sliced

1 cup ricotta

125g mature Cheddar, grated

1 tablespoon Dijon mustard

1 teaspoon salt

3 medium eggs, beaten

VINAIGRETTE

2 tablespoons white-wine vinegar

2 tablespoons extra virgin olive oil

5 tablespoons sunflower oil

2 spring onions, finely sliced

4 tablespoons finely chopped fresh
  basil

salt and black pepper

1   Preheat the oven to 190°C. Butter a large piece of baking paper and line a
    50g loaf tin, leaving enough paper to cover the top. Finely dice half a red
    and half a yellow pepper and set aside. Roughly chop the rest.

2   Heat the oil in a heavy-based saucepan, add the chopped peppers and
    chilli, then cook, covered, for 20 minutes or until softened. Purée in a food
    processor or with a hand blender, then press through a sieve. Combine the
    ricotta, Cheddar, mustard, salt and eggs, then stir in the purée and diced
    peppers. Pour into the tin, then fold the paper over to cover the terrine without
    touching. Place in a roasting pan.

3   Pour in enough boiling water to reach halfway up the sides of the loaf tin,
    then cook for 1 hour 15 minutes, adding more water if necessary. Cool for
    2 hours, then place in the refrigerator for 1 hour. Invert onto a plate and peel
    off the paper.

4   To make the vinaigrette combine the ingredients, mixing well. Serve the terrine
    in slices with the vinaigrette.

Serves 6

Broccoli Soufflés with Olive Purée

(see photograph opposite)

butter for greasing

500g broccoli, chopped

1 cup light cream

4 medium eggs, separated

salt and black pepper

OLIVE PURÉE

20 pitted black olives

½ cup olive oil

grated zest and juice of 1 lemon

1 Preheat the oven to 220°C. Grease four individual ramekin dishes. Cook the broccoli in a little boiling salted water for 15 minutes until tender, then drain well. Blend to a smooth purée with the cream, egg yolks and seasoning in a food processor. Transfer to a large mixing bowl.

2 Beat the egg whites until they increase in volume 6-fold and form soft peaks. Gently fold a third of the beaten whites into the broccoli purée, using a large metal spoon. Carefully fold in the remaining whites in 2 batches, mixing well.

3 Divide the mixture between the ramekin dishes and cook for 20–25 minutes, until risen and golden. Meanwhile, purée the olives, olive oil and lemon zest and juice in a food processor or with a hand blender. Serve with the soufflés.

Serves 4

Note: This method of making soufflés is easier than most. They may not rise as much, but they're unlikely to be a disaster! The olive purée gives them a rich taste. Serve with crusty French bread.

Chilli Broccoli Spread

(see photograph page 8)

3 cloves garlic

500g broccoli

1 tablespoon olive oil

¼ teaspoon chilli powder

⅔ cup boiling water

salt

bruschetta or crostini

3 to 4 black olives

1 Crush and peel garlic and chop finely. Trim broccoli and cut into florets.

2 Heat oil in a saucepan. Saute garlic over a low heat for 2 minutes. Add chilli powder and saute for a further 1 minute or until garlic and chilli are fragrant. Add broccoli, water and salt. Cover and cook over a medium heat for about 10 minutes or until broccoli is just cooked. Remove lid.

3 Mash with a potato masher. Continue to cook over a low heat, mashing regularly, until water has evaporated and broccoli has formed a coarse puree. Use to top bruschetta or crostini and garnish with sliced black olives.

Makes 1½ cups

Baby Squash with Pepper and Cheese Filling

(see photograph page 9)

24 yellow baby squash

1 large pepper, finely chopped

60g tasty cheese, grated

1 egg, lightly beaten

2 spring onions, finely chopped

¼ teaspoon cayenne pepper

1 Cook squash in boiling water until tender, then drain and cool. Scoop out top part of each squash.

2 Combine pepper, cheese, egg, spring onions and cayenne pepper. Spoon into squash.

3 Bake in a moderate oven for 10 minutes or until heated through. Serve.

Makes 24

Asparagus with Vinaigrette

1 tablespoon Dijon mustard

4 tablespoons red-wine vinegar

1 teaspoon sugar

½ teaspoon salt

½ teaspoon ground black pepper

finely chopped parsley and snipped
  fresh chives to taste

½ cup olive oil

1 bunch asparagus

1 For the vinaigrette, measure mustard into bowl. Whisk in vinegar, sugar, salt, pepper and herbs to taste.

2 Continue whisking, slowly adding oil until mixture thickens. Cover until ready to use.

3 Wash asparagus well to remove any grit and snap off the woody ends by bending each spear between your thumb and forefinger. Steam for 5–10 minutes until tender but crisp.

4 Arrange on a plate and drizzle with vinaigrette. Serve warm or cold.

Serves 2–4

Asparagus Polonaise

1 kg fresh asparagus

salt

4 tablespoons butter

45g breadcrumbs, made from
stale bread

3 hard boiled egg yolks, chopped

1 tablespoon chopped fresh parsley

1 First prepare the asparagus. Wash well to remove any grit and snap off the
woody ends by bending each spear between your thumb and forefinger. Peel
the spear two thirds the way up to create a beautiful contrast of pale and
dark greens when cooked. Tie the asparagus into 1–2 bundles. Place any
trimmings and enough boiling salted water in a deep saucepan to fill it by
one third.

2 Stand the asparagus upright in the pan, cover with a lid or dome of
aluminium foil and place over a moderate heat. Bring to the boil, lower the
heat and simmer for 15 minutes or until the asparagus is just tender. Drain
and arrange on a heated serving plate. Keep warm.

3 Heat the butter in a small frying pan over a moderate heat and fry the
breadcrumbs, stirring, until golden. Stir in the egg yolks and parsley, heat
through and spoon over the asparagus. Serve immediately.

Serves 4

Spinach and Ricotta Bake

1 tablespoon olive oil

1 onion, chopped

1 kg frozen whole leaf spinach, defrosted

1 cup ricotta

90g pine nut kernels

¼ teaspoon ground nutmeg

salt and black pepper

6 sheets filo pastry

2 tablespoons olive oil for brushing

1 beaten egg for glazing

1 Preheat the oven to 200°C. Heat the oil in a heavy-based frying pan, add the onion and fry for 3–4 minutes, until slightly softened.

2 Put the spinach into a colander, press to squeeze out any excess water, then roughly chop. Place in a bowl and add the onion, ricotta, pine nuts and nutmeg. Season with salt and plenty of pepper and mix well.

3 Lightly oil a 30 x 25cm ovenproof dish. Add the spinach mixture, pressing down gently to form an even layer. Place a sheet of filo on top, folding it to fit the tin, then lightly brush with oil. Repeat with the remaining filo, brushing each sheet with oil before placing the next on top.

4 Mark the top into 6 portions using a sharp knife, then brush with the egg. Cook for 25 minutes or until golden brown, cut into portions and serve.

Serves 6

Note: This Greek-style bake is a real classic and always goes down well. Add a good helping of mature Cheddar or another hard cheese to the filling for extra punch.

Italian Ribollita

2 onions

2 carrots

2 sticks celery

2 cloves garlic

2 courgettes

250g spinach

6 large tomatoes

2 tablespoons olive oil

3 tablespoons chopped parsley

3 cups water

2 tablespoons tomato purée

salt and pepper

3 slices stale bread

Parmesan cheese

1 Peel onions and carrots and chop very finely. Trim celery. Crush and peel garlic. Chop celery and garlic finely. Trim zucchinis and cut into cubes. Wash spinach and remove stems. Cut tomatoes into cubes, removing the stem end.

2 Heat oil in a large saucepan and add onions, carrots, celery, garlic and parsley. Saute over a medium heat for about 7 minutes or until soft. Add courgettes, spinach and tomatoes to the saucepan with the water and tomato paste. Cover and cook for about 20 minutes or until vegetables are mushy. Season with salt and pepper.

3 Add bread and cook for a further 20 minutes. Thin with hot water if necessary. Serve garnished with Parmesan cheese shavings if wished.

Serves 6

Three C's Carrot Soup

500g carrots

2 onions

2 cloves garlic

2 tablespoons butter

1 teaspoon ground coriander

4 cups vegetarian chicken stock

1 tablespoon sweet chilli sauce

2 large tomatoes

3 tablespoons chopped fresh coriander

1   Scrub or peel carrots. Cut into 3cm lengths. Peel onions and chop roughly. Crush, peel and chop garlic.

2   Melt butter in a large saucepan. Saute onion and garlic over a low heat for 5 minutes or until clear. Add ground coriander and cook for 30 seconds or until it smells fragrant. Pour in stock, bring to boil and add carrots. Cover and cook for 20 minutes or until carrots are tender.

3   Mash with a potato masher. Stir in chilli sauce. Cut tomatoes in half, remove seeds and cut flesh into 1cm cubes. Mix into soup, reserving some for garnish. Stir in chilli sauce and two tablespoons of fresh coriander.

4   Heat through and serve garnished with reserved chopped tomato and coriander.

Serves 4–6

Fresh Vegetable Soup

4 large carrots

2 parsnips

2 leeks

4 zucchinis

1 small head broccoli

8 cups vegetarian chicken stock

salt

freshly ground black pepper

1 Scrub or peel carrots and parsnips and cut into chunks. Trim and wash leeks, then slice thinly. Trim courgettes and slice. Trim broccoli and cut into florets.

2 Bring chicken stock to the boil in a large saucepan. Add vegetables and cook covered for 15 minutes or until vegetables are tender.

3 Season with salt and pepper. Puree if wished or serve chunky.

Serves 4

side dishes

Summer Tabbouleh

(see photograph on page 30)

170g bulgar wheat

2 medium eggs

1 red onion, finely chopped

2 cloves garlic, finely chopped

1 red and 1 yellow pepper, cored, deseeded and finely chopped

1 tablespoon each chopped fresh parsley, chives and coriander

3 tablespoons chopped fresh mint

grated zest and juice of 1 lemon

grated zest and juice of 1 lime

3 tablespoons olive oil

salt and black pepper

1 Prepare the bulgur according to the packet instructions, until tender. Meanwhile, bring a saucepan of water to the boil. Add the eggs and boil for 10 minutes. Cool under cold running water, then remove the shells and mash the eggs.

2 Add the onion, garlic, peppers, parsley, chives, coriander, mint, lemon and lime zest and juice, and the oil to the bulgur, then mix well. Season to taste before serving.

Serves 4

Note: This Middle Eastern dish goes with almost anything. It's particularly good at buffets or barbecues. You can also serve it as a main course with a large salad.

Sweet-and-Sour Red Cabbage

(see photograph opposite)

3 tablespoons olive oil

2 tablespoons red-wine vinegar

1 red or green chilli, sliced, seeds and pith included

grated zest and juice of 1 orange

1 tablespoon orange-flower water

3 tablespoons light brown sugar

1 red cabbage, thinly sliced

1 Preheat the oven to 160°C. Put the oil, vinegar, chilli, orange zest and juice, orange-flower water and sugar into a small saucepan and simmer for 5 minutes.

2 Place the cabbage in an ovenproof casserole dish, then pour over the oil and vinegar mixture, reserving about 2 tablespoons. Cover with a lid or double layer of foil and bake for 3 hours, checking the cabbage every hour, and adding the remaining oil and vinegar mixture if it starts to dry out. Serve hot or cold.

Serves 4

Note: Long, gentle cooking is essential for this dish. It goes particularly well with roast pork, venison and game birds such as pheasant.

Green Beans and Mustard Sauce

500g green beans

3 egg yolks

1 tablespoon French mustard

2 teaspoons butter

¼ cup cream

2 teaspoons vinegar

1 To make the sauce heat the egg yolks, mustard and butter in a double boiler over simmering water. Mix continuously until mixture is frothy.

2 Add cream and mix for 3 minutes. Add vinegar. This can be set aside at this stage and reheated over simmering water when the beans are cooked.

3 Wash and top and tail beans. Steam until tender but still crisp.

4 Pour sauce over beans and serve.

Serves 6

Corn Cobs with Mixed Vegetables in Coconut Cream

4 corn cobs

1 kg mixed vegetables (e.g. French beans, potatoes, butternut pumpkin, carrot, cauliflower, okra)

½ bunch spinach

small bunch coriander leaves

2½ cm piece fresh green ginger

2 green chillies

2 tablespoons oil

2 teaspoons salt

1 teaspoon each ground coriander and cumin

1 cup coconut cream

1 Remove the outside leaves and as much silk as possible from the corn and cut each cob into 4 pieces. Peel and cut the mixed vegetables into chunks or cubes. Remove the white stalks and chop the spinach and coriander. Wash them both and set aside. Place the other vegetables in a colander and wash well. Peel and grate the ginger. Seed and chop the chillies.

2 Heat the oil in a large heavy saucepan. Add the ginger and chillies and stir in the corn pieces. Scatter over half the chopped spinach and coriander, spoon in all the vegetables and scatter over the remaining spinach and coriander.

3 Add the salt, ground coriander and cumin to the coconut cream and pour half over the vegetables. Cover with a tight-fitting lid and simmer very gently for 10–15 minutes or until vegetables are cooked but still crisp. Remove the lid and add the remaining coconut cream.

4 Serve immediately. Garnish with fresh coriander, if desired.

Serves 4–6

Celery Root and Herb Rémoulade

2 medium eggs

500g celery root, grated

2 tablespoons olive oil

1 tablespoon sesame oil

juice of 1 lemon

3 tablespoons chopped fresh parsley

3 tablespoons snipped fresh chives

salt and black pepper

1 Bring a saucepan of water to the boil. Add the eggs and boil for 10 minutes. Cool under cold running water, then remove the shells and finely chop the eggs.

2 Place the celery root and chopped eggs in a large bowl. Mix together the olive oil, sesame oil and lemon juice and pour over the celery root and eggs. Add the parsley, chives and seasoning, then mix thoroughly.

Serves 4

Note: On a hot summer's day, this salad makes a great starter or side dish. The nutty flavours of the celeriac and sesame oil are set off by plenty of lemon juice and fresh herbs.

Brussels Sprouts with Horseradish

750g Brussels sprouts

3 large carrots

3 leeks, washed

2 tablespoons butter

3 teaspoons horseradish cream

3 tablespoons cider vinegar

1 teaspoon parsley flakes

1 teaspoon dill leaf tips

½ teaspoon salt

ground black pepper to taste

1 Trim outer leaves of Brussels sprouts. Cut carrots into 2cm slices and leeks into 1cm pieces. Steam all vegetables until tender (10–12 minutes). Drain. Meanwhile, melt butter in a heavy saucepan. Stir in the remaining ingredients. Toss well with hot vegetables and serve immediately.

Serves 4

Spicy Cauliflower and Potato

3 tablespoons vegetable oil

1 teaspoon black mustard seeds

½ teaspoon whole cumin seeds

1 teaspoon freshly chopped chilli

1 teaspoon freshly crushed garlic

½ teaspoon freshly chopped ginger

1 teaspoon ground turmeric

1 teaspoon ground cumin

500g cauliflower, cut into florets

500g potato, peeled, cut into 2cm dice

¼ cup water

½ cup vegetable stock

1 Heat oil in a wok or frypan. Fry seeds until they begin to pop. Add chilli, garlic, ginger, turmeric and ground cumin and cook for 1 minute, stirring.

2 Add potato, cook for a few minutes, then add cauliflower and water. Cover and cook for 10 minutes or until the vegetables are cooked.

3 Transfer to a serving dish. Add stock to pan and cook until reduced by half. Pour over cauliflower and potato and serve.

Serves 4–6

Parsnip and Carrot Bake

60g butter

2 cloves garlic, crushed

500g parsnip, washed and grated

350g carrot, peeled and grated

1 teaspoon rosemary leaves

1 teaspoon parsley flakes

ground black pepper to taste

1¼ cups cream

1½ cups fresh breadcrumbs

3 tablespoons Parmesan cheese, grated

1 Preheat oven to 200°C.

2 Melt butter in a large frypan. Cook garlic 1 minute. Add parsnip and carrot and cook over medium heat, stirring occasionally, until almost cooked.

3 Season with rosemary, parsley and pepper.

4 Transfer to greased shallow ovenproof dish and pour over cream. Sprinkle with breadcrumbs and cheese and dot with butter. Bake in oven for 35 minutes or until browned.

Serves 4

Red Cabbage with Apple and Walnuts

1 red cabbage

¼ cup vinegar

1 teaspoon sugar

salt to taste

freshly ground black pepper to taste

2 onions, sliced

½ cup olive oil

2 cloves

1 bay leaf

⅓ cup vegetable stock

2 apples, peeled and sliced

grated zest of 1 orange

200g walnut halves

1   Halve the cabbage, discard stalk, wash and slice.

2   Place the vinegar, sugar, salt and pepper in a large dish. Add the cabbage. Mix and soak for 30 minutes.

3   Fry the onion in the oil in a large saucepan. Layer with cabbage. Add cloves, bay leaf, orange zest and pour stock over. Cover and cook over low heat for 2 hours. Add water if it begins to dry out.

4   Add the apples and the walnuts 30 minutes before cooking is complete. Do not stir.

5   Remove bay leaf before serving.

Serves 6–8

Harvard Beets

1 kg beetroot, well rinsed

½ cup sugar

5 tablespoons red-wine vinegar

¼ cup fresh orange juice

2 teaspoons cornflour

salt to taste

freshly ground black pepper to taste

1 tablespoon butter

grated zest of 2 oranges

1 Place beets in a saucepan, cover with cold water and bring to the boil. Reduce heat to a simmer, cover and cook for 40–50 minutes or until tender. Drain and rinse under cold water to cool.

2 Remove skins and cut into ½cm dice. There should be 4 cups of beet. Place in a serving bowl.

3 Combine sugar, vinegar, orange juice, cornflour, salt and pepper in a saucepan. Whisk well and bring to the boil over a medium heat, whisking constantly until the mixture is clear and thickened, about 4–5 minutes.

4 Whisk in the butter and zest. Cook until butter has melted. Remove from heat.

5 Pour sauce over beetroot. Toss. Serve hot or at room temperature.

Serves 6

Deep-Fried Snake Beans

2 cups vegetable oil for deep frying

500g snake beans, cut into
  short lengths

1 tablespoon finely chopped garlic

1 tablespoon finely chopped fresh
  ginger

2 tablespoons finely chopped spring
  onions

2 dried red chillies (optional)

1 tablespoon Chinese rice wine or dry
  sherry

1 tablespoon soy sauce

1 tablespoon sugar

1 tablespoon water

1. Heat the oil in a wok or a deep, heavy-based frying pan until a single bean dropped in sizzles all over. Add half the beans to pan and deep fry for 3–4 minutes or until slightly wrinkled. Using a slotted spoon, remove and drain on paper towels. Repeat with the remaining beans.

2. Remove the oil from the pan, wipe clean with paper towels and return to a high heat. Add 1 tablespoon of oil to the pan, add the garlic, ginger, spring onions and chillies (if using), and stir-fry for 30 seconds or until the chillies blacken. Discard the chillies.

3. Add to the pan the wine or sherry, soy sauce, sugar and water and stir-fry for 2–3 seconds. Return the beans to the pan, heat through and serve immediately.

Serves 4–6

Olla Gitana (Gypsy Stew)

2 medium-sized aubergines

4 onions

2 green or red peppers

3 cloves garlic

4 tomatoes

salt and black pepper

½ cup olive oil

½ cup black olives to garnish

½ cup chopped parsley to garnish

1   Cut the unpeeled aubergines into cubes, sprinkle with salt and leave for 1 hour. Rinse and pat dry with paper towels. Slice or quarter the onions and quarter the peppers, removing the seeds and membranes. Chop the garlic and cut the tomatoes into thick slices.

2   In a medium-sized saucepan, arrange in separate layers the onions, peppers, garlic, aubergine and lastly the tomatoes, sprinkling each layer with salt and pepper to taste. Pour the oil over vegetables. Cover and simmer gently for 40 minutes. Serve topped with olives and parsley.

Serves 6

Note: When buying vegetables for this dish look for tiny purple and white aubergine (smaller than a golf ball) baby fresh onions, bright red capsicums and small egg tomatoes. The vegetables are so young and tender they can be cooked whole (peppers quartered).

Brussels Sprouts with Almond Pesto

(see photograph opposite, left)

500g Brussels sprouts

¼ cup almond pesto

¼ cup toasted flaked almonds

ALMOND PESTO

¾ cup tightly packed fresh basil

1 clove garlic

pinch salt

¼ cup olive oil

½ cup toasted almonds

2 tablespoons grated Parmesan cheese

1 Wash and trim Brussels sprouts. Cut a cross in the stem end of the sprouts. Steam, boil or microwave sprouts until just tender. Drain well. Toss through pesto and garnish with toasted flaked almonds.

ALMOND PESTO

1 Place basil in a bowl of a food processor or in a mortar. Crush and peel the garlic. Add to basil with the salt and half the oil. Process or pound with a pestle to a smooth paste. Add almonds and remaining oil and process or pound until the nuts are lightly chopped. Mix in Parmesan cheese.

Serves 4

Courgette and Mint Moulds with Fresh Tomato Sauce

(see photograph opposite, right)

If mint is not available, use fresh basil.

6 courgettes

1 tablespoon salt

1 tablespoon chopped fresh mint

1 tablespoon chopped fresh chives or spring onions

freshly ground black pepper

1 tomato

FRESH TOMATO SAUCE

6 tomatoes

1 onion

2 cloves garlic

1 tablespoon oil

¼ cup chopped fresh basil

1 Trim courgettes and grate coarsely. Place in a sieve and mix through salt. Leave to drain for 30 minutes to 1 hour.

2 Squeeze courgettes and mix with mint, chives or spring onions and pepper. Cut tomato in half and remove seeds. Cut flesh into 5mm dice. Mix through courgettes.

3 Pack corgette mixture into six small ramekins. Refrigerate until ready to serve. Serve with fresh tomato sauce.

FRESH TOMATO SAUCE

1 Cut tomatoes in half. Remove core and chop flesh roughly. Peel onion and chop finely. Crush, peel and chop garlic.

2 Heat oil in a saucepan. Saute onion and garlic for 5 minutes or until clear not coloured. Add tomatoes and basil and cook for 5 minutes, breaking tomatoes up with a wooden spoon.

3 Leave chunky or puree in a sieve or blender. Serve warm or cold.

Serves 4

Ratatouille

(see photograph opposite)

1 aubergine

salt

1 onion

3 cloves garlic

1 tablespoon oil

1 tablespoon tomato purée

4 tomatoes

1 red pepper

1 green pepper

4 courgettes

1 teaspoon dried rosemary

½ teaspoon thyme

1 bay leaf

1 tablespoon chopped parsley

1 Trim ends from aubergine. Cut into slices and sprinkle with salt. Set aside while preparing remaining ingredients. Peel and finely chop onions. Crush, peel and chop garlic.

2 Heat oil in a frying pan or flameproof casserole dish. Saute onion and garlic for 3 to 5 minutes, or until onion is clear. Mix onion, garlic and tomato paste together in the casserole dish. Dice the tomatoes. Deseed and slice the red and green peppers. Trim the courgettes and cut into 1cm slices. Add tomatoes, peppers, courgette, rosemary, thyme and bay leaf to casserole dish. Wash salt from aubergine and cut each slice into quarters. Add to casserole dish. Mix gently. Cover and cook at 180°C for 1 to 1¼ hours. Serve sprinkled with chopped parsley.

Serves 4–6

Note: Anyone who has discovered this delicious vegetable combination has their own special blend. This is mine. Feel free to experiment with your own brew depending on what is in season at the right price.

Vegetable Curry

500g mixed fresh seasonal vegetables
such as pumpkin, parsnip, broccoli,
beans, etc.

2 onions

1 tablespoon oil

1 tablespoon curry powder

400ml can coconut cream

1 tablespoon sweet chilli sauce

1 tablespoon soy sauce

2 tablespoons chopped fresh coriander

1 tablespoon chopped fresh basil

1 Prepare the vegetables, peeling, trimming and chopping as necessary. Cut into even-sized pieces. Peel onions and chop finely.

2 Heat oil in a saucepan and saute onion for 5 minutes. Add curry powder and saute for 1 minute. Mix in coconut cream. Bring to the boil. Add vegetables. Cover and simmer until vegetables are tender. Mix in chilli and soy sauce.

3 Serve garnished with coriander and basil.

Serves 4–6

Note: Serve this with plain grilled or barbecued meats to add interest to any everyday meal.

Broccoli with Lemon Yoghurt Sauce

500g broccoli

1 onion

2 cloves garlic

1 tablespoon olive oil

1 teaspoon grated lemon rind

2 teaspoons French mustard

¾ cup natural unsweetened yoghurt

salt

freshly ground black pepper

1   Wash broccoli. Trim and cut in even-sized florets. Steam, boil or microwave until tender. Drain. While broccoli is cooking, peel onion and chop finely. Crush, peel and chop garlic.

2   Heat oil in a saucepan and saute onion and garlic for 5 minutes or until soft but not coloured. Add lemon rind, mustard, yoghurt and salt to onion mixture and bring to the boil. Do not boil.

3   Place broccoli in a serving dish and pour over yoghurt mixture. Grind over black pepper. Serve immediately.

Serves 4

main courses

Roasted Vegetable and Broccoli Couscous

(see photograph on page 50)

4 parsnips, cut into chunks

2 sweet potatoes, cut into chunks

4 turnips, quartered

2 cloves garlic, crushed

6 tablespoons olive oil

salt

5 tablespoons apple or redcurrant jelly

300g couscous

500g tomatoes, chopped

handful each of chopped fresh parsley, chives and basil

juice of 1 lemon

300g broccoli, cut into florets

1 Preheat the oven to 200°C. Cook the parsnips in a saucepan of boiling salted water for 2 minutes, then drain. Place in a roasting pan with the sweet potatoes, turnips, garlic and 3 tablespoons of oil, turning to coat. Sprinkle with salt, then cook for 30 minutes or until lightly browned.

2 Melt the apple or redcurrant jelly in a pan with 4 tablespoons of water for 2–3 minutes, until it turns syrupy. Turn the vegetables in the tin and carefully spoon over the syrup. Return to the oven for 10 minutes or until browned and glossy.

3 Meanwhile, prepare the couscous according to the packet instructions. Heat the rest of the oil in a frying pan and cook the tomatoes for 2–3 minutes, until softened. Add the couscous and heat through, then mix in the herbs and lemon juice. Meanwhile, boil the broccoli florets for 2 minutes or until tender, then drain. Serve the couscous with the roasted vegetables and broccoli arranged on top.

Serves 6

Note: When they're roasted, vegetables caramelise naturally. Glazing them with apple or redcurrant jelly adds extra gloss and makes them taste even sweeter.

Tortilla with Corn and Sun-Dried Tomatoes

(see photograph opposite)

250g potatoes, thickly sliced

3 tablespoons olive oil

3 tablespoons canned corn, drained

4 sun-dried tomatoes in oil, drained and chopped

2 tablespoons chopped fresh parsley

6 medium eggs, beaten

salt and black pepper

1 Boil the potatoes for 10 minutes and leave to cool slightly. Heat the oil in a large, flameproof, heavy-based frying pan, add the potatoes and fry over a high heat for 2–3 minutes, until browned and crisp. Reduce the heat, then stir in the corn and tomatoes and heat through for 1–2 minutes.

2 Preheat the grill to medium. Add the parsley to the eggs and season, then pour over the vegetables in the frying pan. Cook over a low heat for 3–4 minutes, until the omelette base is set and lightly browned.

3 Place the pan under the grill for 1–2 minutes, until the top is set and golden. Leave to cool slightly, then cut into 4 wedges and serve with salad.

Serves 4

Note: You can choose any combination of vegetables and herbs you like for this Spanish-style omelette, but make quite sure the potato is crisp and golden before pouring in the egg.

Fusilli with Aubergine and Tomatoes

2 medium aubergine

½ cup olive oil

1 clove garlic

4 medium tomatoes

salt and pepper

2 tablespoons chopped basil leaves

2 tablespoons Parmesan cheese, grated

300g fusilli (spirals)

freshly ground black pepper

1 Peel aubergine and cut into small dice.

2 Pour half the oil into a frying pan and add the garlic and diced aubergine. Fry gently until tender.

3 Meanwhile, skin the tomatoes, remove the seeds and dice the flesh.

4 Pour the remaining oil into the frying pan and add the diced tomatoes. Cook for about 5 minutes and add salt, pepper and basil.

5 Meanwhile cook the fusilli in boiling, salted water for 10–12 minutes until al dente. Drain. Toss in the aubergine and tomatoes. Sprinkle with Parmesan and black pepper, mix and serve.

Serves 4

Roman Stuffed Tomatoes*

6 large tomatoes

1½ cups cooked long-grain rice
 (⅔ cup uncooked)

2 tablespoons chopped basil leaves

¼ cup olive oil

4 canned anchovy fillets, drained
 and chopped

2 cloves garlic, crushed

1 teaspoon sugar

salt and freshly ground black pepper

*This recipe contains anchovy fillets

1 Preheat oven to 190°C. Slice the caps off the tomatoes and set aside. Use a teaspoon to scoop some of the flesh out of each tomato, leaving a thick shell. Roughly chop the inside tomato flesh and mix it with the remaining ingredients, seasoning with salt and pepper.

2 Stand the tomatoes in an oiled shallow ovenproof dish just large enough to hold them in one layer and fill them with the rice mixture. Top with the caps.

3 Bake in a moderately hot oven for 15 minutes, basting with cooking juices every now and then.

4 Serve hot or at room temperature.

Serves 6

Italian Spinach Tart

(see photograph opposite)

PASTRY

2 cups plain flour

pinch salt

125g sweet butter

⅓ cup iced water

FILLING

500g spinach

200g fresh ricotta cheese

4 eggs, beaten

60g Parmesan cheese, grated

grated nutmeg

salt and freshly ground black pepper

1 Sift the flour and salt into a large bowl. Cut the butter into small pieces, adding it to the flour. Rub the butter into the flour with your fingertips until the mixture resembles breadcrumbs. Don't overdo this as the butter will be blended more thoroughly later.

2 Make a well in the centre. Mix in the iced water and combine quickly with a knife. Press the dough together with your fingers.

3 Turn out on to a floured board and knead lightly until smooth. Roll into a ball. Brush off excess flour. Wrap in waxed paper and refrigerate for 20–30 minutes before using.

4 Preheat oven to 200°C. Roll out the pastry and use it to line a 25cm flan ring. Trim the edges. Prick the base lightly with a fork and line with baking paper. Half fill with dried beans and bake 'blind' in a preheated hot oven for 7 minutes. Remove the beans and bake for a further 5 minutes.

5 Meanwhile, wash the spinach and place it in a saucepan with the water clinging to the leaves. Cook, covered, until tender. Then drain, squeeze dry, cool and chop finely. In a bowl, beat the ricotta until smooth, then beat in the eggs, Parmesan, nutmeg and spinach. Season the mixture and pour it into the prebaked pastry shell. Reduce oven temperature and bake in a moderate oven 180°C for 25–30 minutes until golden and set. Serve cold.

Serves 4

Mushroom and Black Olive Risotto

30g dried porcini mushrooms

3 tablespoons olive oil

1 onion, chopped

250g large open mushrooms, chopped

250g arborio rice

2 cups vegetable stock

2 tablespoons black olives, pitted and
 roughly chopped

salt and black pepper

2 tablespoons black olive paste

fresh Parmesan cheese to serve

1 Cover the porcini with 200ml of boiling water, then leave to soak for
 20 minutes. Drain, reserving the water, and set aside. Heat the oil in a
 large heavy-based saucepan, add the onion and fresh mushrooms and fry for
 4–5 minutes. Add the rice and stir to coat with the oil. Fry for 1–2 minutes.

2 Add the porcini and the reserved liquid to the rice with 1 cup of the
 vegetable stock and the olives. Simmer, covered, for 10 minutes or until the
 liquid has been absorbed, stirring occasionally.

3 Stir in half of the remaining stock and cook for 5 minutes, covered, until
 absorbed. Add the rest of the stock, the seasoning and the olive paste and
 cook for 5 minutes, uncovered, stirring constantly. Remove from the heat and
 leave to rest, covered, for 5 minutes. Shave the Parmesan, using a vegetable
 peeler, and sprinkle over risotto then serve.

Serves 4

Spinach and Roquefort Tart

340g shortcrust pastry, thawed if frozen

250g fresh spinach, thick stalks discarded

black pepper

pinch of freshly grated nutmeg

125g Roquefort or other blue cheese, cubed

1 medium egg, beaten

1¼ cups light cream

1 Preheat the oven to 200°C. Roll out the pastry on a lightly floured surface and use it to line a 23cm flan dish. Prick the pastry base with a fork and bake for 10 minutes or until lightly golden.

2 Meanwhile, rinse the spinach and place it in a saucepan with the water clinging to its leaves. Cook, covered, for 3–4 minutes, until wilted. Drain, leave to cool slightly, then squeeze out the excess water. Spoon the spinach into the pastry base and spread with the back of a wooden spoon. Season with pepper and nutmeg, then add the cheese. Mix together the egg and cream and pour over the top.

3 Bake for 30 minutes or until the filling has risen and is golden. Leave to rest for 10 minutes before serving in slices.

Serves 6

Note: Blue cheese and cream make this spinach tart rich but irresistible. Make sure any excess water is squeezed out of the spinach for a good firm texture.

Spinach Lasagne

(see photograph opposite, top)

500g spinach

1 onion

2 cloves garlic

2 tablespoons butter

½ teaspoon salt

250g pot low fat sour cream

pinch nutmeg

250g packet fresh egg lasagne

100g pot sundried tomato pesto

3 tomatoes

100g mozzarella cheese

1 Wash spinach and trim. Place in a saucepan with only the water clinging to the leaves and cook for 3 to 5 minutes. Drain well and squeeze out as much water as possible. Chop spinach finely. Peel onion and chop finely. Crush, peel and chop garlic.

2 Melt butter in a saucepan and saute onion and garlic for 3 to 5 minutes or until soft. Remove from heat and stir in spinach, salt, sour cream and nutmeg.

3 Cut lasagne to fit a 16 x 37cm lasagne dish. Spread a sheet of lasagne with tomato pesto then a layer of spinach mixture. Repeat layering until ingredients are used up, finishing with a layer of pesto-spread lasagne.

4 Cut tomatoes and cheese into 1cm cubes, removing the cores from tomatoes. Arrange over top sheet of lasagne. Bake at 180°C for 10 to 15 minutes or until heated through.

Serves 4

Quick Calzone

(see photograph opposite, bottom)

2 large pitta bread rounds

4 courgettes

2 red peppers

10 mushrooms

2 tablespoons vegetable oil

1 tablespoon capers

2 tablespoons sundried tomato pesto

2 tablespoons grated Parmesan cheese

1 Cut through top layer of pitta bread through the centre from edge to edge. Turn and cut at right angles to the first cut. Trim courgettes. Cut in half lengthwise, then into 4cm chunks. Core peppers and cut flesh into eights. Wipe mushrooms and cut in half if large.

2 Place vegetables on a baking tray and brush with oil. Grill vegetables until courgettes are lightly golden and pepper is blistered. Place vegetables in a bowl and mix in capers and sundried tomato pesto.

3 Carefully open the pitta breads along the cuts and fill with the vegetable mixture. Brush cut top of pitas with oil and sprinkle with Parmesan cheese.

4 Bake at 200°C for 10 minutes or until heated through. Serve cut into wedges.

Serves 4–6

Note: Use grated tasty cheese instead of Parmesan if preferred.

Tuscan Vegetable Terrine

(see photograph opposite)

300g pumpkin, peeled

olive oil for brushing

16 plum tomatoes

400g Bocconcini cheese, well-drained

1 bunch fresh basil

freshly ground black pepper

1 bunch rocket

MUSTARD AND BALSAMIC DRESSING

1 teaspoon wholegrain mustard

2 tablespoons balsamic vinegar

2 tablespoons olive oil

Italian bread

1 Preheat oven to 180°C. Line a terrine or loaf dish with plastic food wrap, leaving enough to cover top of terrine overhanging the sides. Set aside.

2 Cut pumpkin into 1cm-thick slices to fit shape of terrine – there should be enough for a single layer in the terrine. Lightly spray or brush slices with olive oil. Place on a baking tray. Bake for 20–30 minutes or until pumpkin is cooked, but still firm. Cool.

3 Cut tomatoes in half lengthwise. Remove seeds and press gently with hands to flatten. Cut cheese into 5mm thick slices.

4 Layer the ingredients in the terrine in the following order: tomatoes, basil leaves, cheese, tomatoes, basil leaves, cheese, pumpkin, basil leaves, tomatoes, cheese, basil leaves, tomatoes and finally cheese. The overall effect should be layers of tomatoes, basil and cheese with a layer of pumpkin in the centre. When layering, place the tomatoes skin side down and season each tomato layer with a little black pepper. Cover terrine with the overhanging plastic wrap. Weigh down. Refrigerate overnight.

5 To make the dressing, place mustard, vinegar and oil in a screwtop jar. Shake well to combine. Set aside until ready to use.

6 To serve, using the plastic wrap, carefully lift terrine from dish. Cut into thick slices. Line serving plates with rocket leaves. Place a slice of terrine on top. Drizzle with dressing. Serve with Italian bread.

Serves 8

Vegetable Cannelloni

(see photograph opposite)

12 instant (no precooking required)
 cannelloni tubes

250g mozzarella cheese, grated

LEEK AND SPINACH FILLING

2 teaspoons olive oil

1 clove garlic, crushed

2 spring onions, finely chopped

2 leeks, thinly sliced

1 red pepper, sliced

1 bunch English spinach, chopped

200g ricotta cheese, drained

315g canned creamed corn

2 teaspoons ground paprika

TOMATO SAUCE

1 teaspoon olive oil

1 onion, chopped

400g canned tomato purée

2 tablespoons dry white wine

1 To make filling, heat oil in a frying pan over a medium heat. Add garlic, spring onions and leeks and cook, stirring, for 4 minutes or until leeks are soft.

2 Add red pepper and spinach and cook, stirring, for 3 minutes or until spinach wilts. Drain off liquid.

3 Transfer vegetable mixture to a large bowl, add ricotta cheese, corn and paprika and mix well to combine.

4 Spoon filling into cannelloni tubes and place tubes side-by-side in a greased large ovenproof dish. Set aside.

5 To make sauce, heat oil in a saucepan over a medium heat. Add onion and cook, stirring, for 3 minutes or until onion is soft. Stir in tomato purée and wine, bring to simmering and simmer for 4 minutes. Pour sauce over cannelloni tubes, sprinkle with mozzarella cheese and bake for 40 minutes or until pasta is tender and cheese is golden. Add serving instructions.

Serves 4

Mixed-Mushroom and Goat's-Cheese Strudel

(see photograph opposite)

1 teaspoon extra virgin olive oil

2 spring onions, finely diced

2 cloves garlic, crushed

500g mixed mushrooms of your choice
   (e.g. shiitake, Swiss or oyster), diced

½ cup white wine

1 teaspoon lemon juice

90g reduced-fat feta cheese, crumbled

3 tablespoons chopped fresh mixed
   herbs (e.g. sage, thyme, oregano,
   rosemary)

8 sheets filo pastry

freshly ground black pepper

DRIED-MUSHROOM AND HERB BROTH

2 cups water

1 cup dried mushrooms

2 tablespoons tomato purée

1 tablespoon chopped fresh herbs (e.g.
   parsley, basil, chives or coriander)

1 tablespoon sherry

1   Heat the oil in a frying pan over a low heat. Add the onions and garlic. Cook, stirring, for 2–3 minutes or until soft and translucent. Add the mushrooms. Cook, stirring occasionally, for 5–8 minutes or until juices evaporate. Stir in the wine and lemon juice. Cook, stirring occasionally, until liquid is absorbed. Cool.

2   Preheat the oven to 180°C. Lightly spray or brush a baking tray with olive oil or line with nonstick baking paper. Set aside.

3   Stir the cheese and fresh herbs into mushroom mixture. Lay 2 sheets of filo pastry on a clean, dry work surface. Lightly spray or brush with olive oil and season with pepper. Place 2 more sheets on top. Place half the mushroom mixture along the long edge leaving a 3cm border at each end. Fold in the ends. Roll up tightly. Place strudel seam down on prepared baking tray. Repeat with remaining filo and mushroom mixture to make a second strudel. Using a sharp knife, make slashes in the top of each strudel to mark slices. Bake for 10–12 minutes or until golden.

4   To make the broth, place the water in a saucepan and bring to the boil. Add mushrooms, tomato purée, herbs and sherry. Boil until the mushrooms are tender and the mixture starts to thicken.

5   Cut the strudels where marked. Serve with or without broth.

Makes 2 strudels – each cuts into 4 thick slices

Mushroom Lasagne

(see photograph opposite)

3 tablespoons olive oil

2 cloves garlic, crushed

1 kg white mushrooms, finely sliced

6 tablespoons chopped fresh parsley

1 teaspoon chopped fresh oregano or
¼ teaspoon dried

salt and black pepper

250g fresh pasta, cut into flat sheets, or
8 lasagne sheets

150g freshly grated Parmesan cheese

BECHAMEL SAUCE

60g sweet butter

1 small onion, finely chopped

4 tablespoons plain flour

4 cups hot milk

salt

freshly ground black pepper

1 large egg yolk

1   To make the sauce, melt butter in a large saucepan over a moderate heat and cook the onion, stirring, for 5 minutes or until soft. Stir in the flour and cook for 1 minute. Remove the pan from the heat and gradually blend in the milk. Cook, stirring constantly, until the sauce boils and thickens. Season with salt and black pepper. Lower the heat and simmer gently for 10 minutes.

2   Whisk the egg yolk in a small bowl until smooth. Stir a little hot sauce into yolk, then return the mixture to the saucepan. Cook over a low heat, stirring, for 30 seconds. Remove the pan from the heat and keep warm.

3   To make the lasagne, heat the oil in a frying pan over a moderate heat and cook the garlic, stirring, until soft. Add the mushrooms to pan, increase the heat and cook, stirring, until golden. Stir in the herbs. Lower the heat and cook for 10 minutes or until the liquid almost evaporates. Remove from the heat and season with salt and pepper.

4   Preheat the oven to 200°C. Line a buttered 20 x 25cm baking dish with a third of the pasta pieces, overlapping slightly. Spread with ⅓ of the mushroom mixture, top with ⅓ of the sauce and sprinkle with a third of the Parmesan. Repeat this process twice. Bake for 25–30 minutes or until bubbly and golden.

Serves 6

Note: If using dried lasagne sheets, partially cook them beforehand in a large saucepan of boiling salted water to which 1 tablespoon of oil has been added for 3–5 minutes or until pliable. Drain and cool slightly.

salads

Courgette and Hazelnut Salad

(see photograph on page 70)

700g small courgettes

2 tablespoons sunflower oil, plus extra for frying

5 tablespoons walnut oil

1 tablespoon white-wine vinegar

salt and black pepper

125g whole blanched hazelnuts

170g watercress, thick stalks removed

90g feta, crumbled

1 Pare the courgettes lengthwise into slivers using a vegetable peeler. In a bowl, mix together the oils and vinegar, and season. Add half the courgette slivers to the mixture, toss lightly and set aside.

2 Brush a large frying pan with a little sunflower oil and heat. Lay the remaining courgette slivers in the pan and cook for 2 minutes on each side or until lightly charred. Remove, season and set aside. Wipe the pan clean.

3 Roughly crush the hazelnuts, using a mortar and pestle, or put them in a plastic bag, seal and crush with a rolling pin. Place in the frying pan and fry for 1–2 minutes, until golden.

4 Divide the watercress between serving plates. Spoon some of the marinated courgettes into the centre, reserving some of the marinade. Scatter over half the toasted hazelnuts and the feta. Arrange the charred courgettes on top, and sprinkle with the rest of the hazelnuts and the reserved marinade.

Serves 6

Note: This salad combines all sorts of flavours and textures: pan-fried courgettes, crumbled feta and toasted hazelnuts. It tastes amazing and is really quick to make.

Lettuce, Avocado and Peanut Salad

(see photograph opposite)

2 crispy lettuces, leaves separated

1 head Belgian endive, leaves separated

2 small ripe avocados, stoned, peeled and cut into chunks

3 spring onions, chopped

3 tablespoons salted peanuts

DRESSING

1 tablespoon lemon juice

1 clove garlic, crushed

3 tablespoons olive oil

2 tablespoons smooth peanut butter

salt and black pepper

1 To make the dressing, put the lemon juice, garlic, oil and peanut butter into a bowl, combine thoroughly and season.

2 Arrange the lettuce leaves, endive and avocados in a large shallow dish. Pour over the dressing and sprinkle with spring onions and peanuts.

Serves 4

Note: Nutty tastes and textures work well with the avocados and bitter-leafed endive in this salad. Serve as a starter with some chilled Chardonnay.

Roasted Pepper Salad*

1 tablespoon vegetable oil for greasing

4 large peppers, red, yellow and green
(if yellow are unavailable use more
red than green)

1 red onion, peeled and cut into thin
slices from top to bottom

8 anchovy fillets, drained (optional)

1 tablespoon capers, drained

¼ cup fresh oregano, chopped

ground black pepper to taste

2 tablespoons balsamic vinegar

2 tablespoons olive oil

*This recipe contains anchovy fillets

1 Preheat oven to 200°C. Brush two oven trays with oil.

2 Cut tops and bottoms off peppers. Cut into quarters lengthwise and flatten on
baking trays, skin side up. Roast for 12–15 minutes or until softened. Put into
a plastic bag and leave to steam for 10 minutes.

3 At the same time, roast the onion on a separate tray until golden. Leave to
cool for about 10 minutes.

4 When peppers are cool enough to handle, skin and cut into large chunky
pieces.

5 Toss peppers and onions together in a shallow serving bowl. Top with
anchovies (optional) and capers.

6 Scatter with oregano and pepper and drizzle with combined oil and vinegar.

Serves 4

Italian Aubergine Salad

1 large aubergine

¼ cup vegetable oil

2 cloves garlic

¼ cup red-wine vinegar

⅓ cup olive oil

⅓ cup chopped parsley

snipped basil leaves or dill

salt and black pepper

1 red pepper

1 spring onion, finely chopped

1 Cut the aubergine into cubes and fry very gently in a covered pan with vegetable oil until the aubergine is pale golden and tender. Allow to cool in a colander to help drain the excess oil.

2 Meanwhile, use a food processor, purée the garlic with the vinegar, olive oil, parsley, basil or dill and salt and pepper to taste.

3 Toss the aubergine in the dressing in a salad bowl. Char the pepper over a gas flame or under a hot griller until the skin is blackened all over. Now scrape away the blackened skin, rinsing frequently in cold water. When all the pepper is peeled, halve it, flick out the seeds and cut the pepper in large chunks. If you prefer, canned pepper (pimientos) can be used instead. Add to the salad and scatter with the onion.

Serves 4

Mushroom and Mange Tout Salad

250g fresh mushrooms

125g mange tout

½ cup mayonnaise

1 tablespoon lime or lemon juice

5 tablespoons light sour cream

1 tablespoon each chopped fresh
  parsley, chervil and snipped chives

salt and freshly ground pepper

1 Slice the mushrooms very finely. String the mange tout, drop into boiling water for about 10 seconds, drain and refresh in cold water. Cut each one into 3 diagonal pieces. Place in a bowl with the mushrooms.

2 In another bowl combine the mayonnaise with the lime or lemon juice, sour cream, herbs and salt and pepper.

3 Fold the dressing into the mushrooms and mange tout. Turn into a serving bowl and garnish with the chives.

Serves 4

Asparagus and Tomato Salad with Cucumber

1 large bunch asparagus

4 small ripe tomatoes

a selection of salad greens

Dressing

1 small cucumber

1 tiny spring onion

salt

freshly ground pepper

2 tablespoons lemon juice

1 tablespoon sour cream

4 tablespoons each salad oil and
   hazelnut or virgin olive oil

2 tablespoons chopped dill

1 First prepare the dressing. Peel the cucumber lightly and remove the seeds.
Cut the cucumber into chunks, roughly chop the spring onion and sprinkle
them both with salt. Leave to drain for 1 hour in a colander. Rinse in cold
water and drain again thoroughly. Purée in a blender or food processor,
add the salt, pepper, lemon juice, sour cream and oils (last), until a smooth
dressing is formed. Add the dill and refrigerate.

2 Prepare and cook the asparagus and cut into 4cm pieces. Peel the tomatoes,
halve them and remove the seeds. Cut each half into strips.

3 Arrange the salad greens on serving plates.

4 Toss the asparagus and tomato in the dressing and arrange on each plate.

Serves 4

American Potato Salad

1 kg new potatoes

salted water

⅓ cup dry white wine

½ cup vinaigrette dressing

1 red onion, sliced into rings

1 stalk celery, sliced

2 dill pickles or gherkins,
  thinly sliced

1 teaspoon capers

4 hard-boiled eggs, peeled and sliced

chopped parsley

salt and freshly ground pepper

1 Scrub and boil the potatoes in salted water until tender . Peel and slice them while still hot and place into a bowl. Sprinkle with wine, turning the potato slices carefully. Next sprinkle with the vinaigrette dressing and add the remaining ingredients. Season with salt and pepper to serve.

Serves 4

Variation with mayonnaise: Follow the recipe and fold in ½ cup of mayonnaise or ¼ cup each sour cream and mayonnaise after adding the dressing and before adding the remaining ingredients. This is easy to do because the potatoes are already oil coated, which also means less mayonnaise is needed.

Idea: An alternative way to serve new potatoes – remove the skin, wash and boil in salted water. Drain and add chopped spring onions some butter and a heaped teaspoon of rolled oats. Toss all together in a pan and cook through.

Celery, Carrot and Apple Salad with Tahini

3 carrots, grated

1 celery heart, thinly sliced

2 eating apples, peeled, cored and
thinly sliced

DRESSING

3 tablespoons lemon juice

1 clove garlic, crushed

2 tablespoons tahini paste

3 tablespoons water

salt

1 To make the dressing, place the lemon juice, garlic, tahini paste and water in
a food processor and blend until smooth. Alternatively, combine with a fork.
Season to taste.

2 Toss together the carrots, celery heart and apples and transfer to individual
serving bowls. Drizzle with dressing.

Serves 4

*Note: A dash of lemon juice adds sharpness to thick tahini paste, which
is made from sesame seeds. With a little crushed garlic, it makes a great
dressing for this colourful salad.*

Spicy Wild-Rice Salad

(see photograph opposite)

400g wild-rice blend (brown and
   wild-rice mix)

2 tablespoons vegetable oil

2 onions, cut into thin wedges

1 teaspoon ground cumin

½ teaspoon ground cinnamon

¼ teaspoon ground cloves

¼ teaspoon ground ginger

2 carrots, thinly sliced

1 teaspoon honey

2 oranges, segmented

90g pistachios, toasted and roughly
   chopped

90g raisins

60g flaked almonds, toasted

3 spring onions, sliced

3 tablespoons chopped fresh dill

DRESSING

1 teaspoon Dijon mustard

½ cup olive oil

¼ cup orange juice

1 tablespoon red-wine vinegar

1   Cook rice in boiling water following packet directions or until tender. Drain well and set aside to cool.

2   Heat oil in a nonstick frying pan over a medium heat, add onions, cumin, cinnamon, cloves and ginger and cook, stirring, for 10 minutes or until onions are soft and slightly caramelised. Add carrots and cook until tender. Stir in honey, then remove from heat and cool slightly.

3   Place rice, carrot mixture, oranges, pistachios, raisins, almonds, spring onions and dill in a bowl and toss to combine.

4   To make dressing, place mustard, oil, orange juice and vinegar in a bowl and whisk to combine. Pour dressing over salad and toss.

Serves 4

Note: If wild-rice blend is unavailable use ¾ cup brown rice and ¼ cup wild rice. The two varieties of rice can be cooked together.

Oriental Coleslaw

1 daikon (white radish)

1 large carrot

½ Chinese cabbage, shredded

¼ red cabbage, shredded

2 spring onions, cut into long thin strips

18 mange tout, cut lengthwise into thin strips

1 cup shredded spinach

½ cup raisins

½ cup slivered unsalted almonds, toasted (optional)

DRESSING

2 tablespoons sesame seeds

3 teaspoons grated fresh ginger or shredded pickled ginger

1 teaspoon sugar

3 tablespoons rice wine or sherry

2 tablespoons rice or wine vinegar

2 teaspoons macadamia or peanut oil

2 teaspoons reduced-salt soy sauce

few drops sesame oil (optional)

1 Using a zester, Japanese grater or sharp knife, cut the daikon and carrot into long thin strips. Place in a large bowl. Add the Chinese and red cabbages, spring onions, mange tout, spinach, raisins and almonds. Toss to combine.

2 To make the dressing, place the sesame seeds in a small saucepan over a medium heat. Cook, shaking the pan frequently, for 2–3 minutes or until the seeds are toasted. Stir in the ginger, sugar, rice wine or sherry, vinegar, macadamia or peanut oil, soy sauce and sesame oil (if using). Remove the pan from the heat. Immediately pour over the salad. Toss to combine.

Serves 6

Bulgar Wheat Salad with Grilled Peppers

250g bulgur wheat

2 yellow peppers, quartered
  and deseeded

250g green beans, halved

2 ripe tomatoes

4 spring onions, sliced

90g brazil nuts, roughly chopped

4 tablespoons chopped fresh parsley

sea salt and freshly ground
  black pepper

DRESSING

4 tablespoons extra virgin olive oil

1 tablespoon wholegrain mustard

1 garlic clove, crushed

1 teaspoon balsamic vinegar

1 teaspoon white-wine vinegar

1 Place the bulgur in a bowl and cover with boiling water to about 2cm above
   the level of the bulgur and leave to soak for 20 minutes. Meanwhile, preheat
   the grill to high. Grill the peppers, skin-side up, for 15–20 minutes, until the
   skin is blistered and blackened all over. Transfer to a plastic bag, seal and
   leave to cool. When cold enough to handle, remove and discard the charred
   skins and roughly chop the flesh.

2 Blanch the beans in boiling water for 3–4 minutes, drain, refresh under cold
   running water and set aside. Put the tomatoes into a bowl, cover with boiling
   water and leave for 30 seconds. Peel, deseed, then roughly chop the flesh.

3 Combine the ingredients for the dressing and mix well. Drain the bulgur
   and transfer to a salad bowl. Add the dressing and toss well. Add the
   vegetables, spring onions, brazil nuts, parsley and seasoning and toss
   together gently to mix.

Serves 4

*Note: This salad is delicious, filling and extremely nutritious. The mustard and
balsamic vinegar in the dressing bring all the other exciting flavours alive.*

Vietnamese Herbed Rice-Noodles with Peanuts and Asparagus

(see photograph opposite)

3 tablespoons rice vinegar

1 tablespoon sugar

1 small Spanish onion, finely sliced

250g dried rice noodles

2 bunches asparagus

⅓ cup chopped mint leaves

⅓ cup chopped coriander leaves

1 continental cucumber, peeled, seeded and thinly sliced

6 spring onions, finely sliced

3 plum tomatoes, finely diced

¾ cup roasted peanuts, lightly crushed

juice of 2 limes

2 teaspoons Thai fish sauce (nam pla)

2 teaspoons olive oil

½ teaspoon chilli flakes

1 First, whisk the vinegar and sugar together and pour over the onion rings. Allow to marinate for 1 hour, tossing frequently.

2 Cook the noodles according to packet directions (usually, rice noodles need only soak in boiling water for 5 minutes; otherwise, boil for 1–2 minutes then drain immediately and rinse under cold water).

3 Cut the tough stalks off the asparagus, and cut the remaining stalks into 2cm lengths. Simmer the asparagus in salted water for 2 minutes until bright green and crisp-tender. Rinse in cold water to refresh.

4 Toss the noodles with the onion/vinegar mixture while the noodles still warm, then using kitchen scissors, cut the noodles into manageable lengths.

5 To the noodles, add the cooked asparagus, and the mint, coriander, cucumber, spring onions, tomatoes and peanuts and toss thoroughly.

6 Whisk the lime juice, fish sauce, oil and chilli flakes together and drizzle over the noodle salad. Serve at room temperature.

Serves 4

Walnut and Apple Coleslaw

(see photograph opposite, top)

½ cabbage

1 apple

1 tablespoon lemon juice

1 clove garlic

¾ cup natural unsweetened yoghurt

2 tablespoons finely chopped mint

1 tablespoon wine vinegar

¼ cup chopped walnuts

1 tablespoon poppy seeds

1 Slice cabbage finely. Polish the apple. Remove core and cut into thin slices. Toss slices in lemon juice. Crush, peel and finely chop garlic. Drain apple, reserving lemon juice.

2 Place cabbage and apple in a bowl. Combine garlic, reserved lemon juice, yoghurt, mint and vinegar. Add to bowl. Toss well to coat.

3 Cover and chill until ready to serve. Mix through walnuts and poppy seeds just before serving.

Serves 6

Caesar Salad

(see photograph opposite, bottom)

4 cloves garlic

¼ cup olive oil

3 cups French bread cubes

2 cos lettuce

½ teaspoon salt

3 tablespoons lemon juice

¼ cup olive oil

½ teaspoon Worcestershire sauce

3 lightly boiled eggs

½ cup grated or shaved Parmesan cheese

8 anchovy fillets

1 Crush and peel the garlic. Mash two cloves of garlic and mix with first measure of olive oil. Mix well so garlic flavours oil.

2 Pour into a roasting dish, add bread cubes and toss well to coat. Bake at 190°C for 10 to 15 minutes or until golden, turning occasionally.

3 Wash and dry lettuce. Tear leaves into pieces and place in a bowl. Mash remaining garlic with salt. Mix garlic, lemon juice, second measure of olive oil and Worcestershire sauce together. Pour over lettuce. Shell eggs and chop roughly. Sprinkle over Parmesan cheese and toss to mix. Cut anchovies into pieces and place on top of salad with croutons.

Serves 4–6

Note: This makes my mouth water at the thought of it. Serve as a light luncheon meal or as a vegetable accompaniment. The name of this salad has nothing to do with Roman times but was first made in Tijuana, Mexico, at Caesar's Palace, by Italian immigrant, Caesar Cordini. It soon crossed the Mexican border and became an American classic.

Green Bean Salad

500g green beans

2 rashers vegetarian bacon

1 red onion

¼ cup chopped fresh chives

2 tablespoons chopped fresh sage

3 tablespoons white vinegar

¼ cup olive oil

salt

freshly ground black pepper

1 Top and tail beans. Cut in half if they are long. Cook in boiling water for 10 minutes or until just tender. Drain and refresh under cold water. Drain well.

2 Derind bacon and chop flesh finely. Saute in a frying pan for 5 minutes. Peel onion and cut into rings. Add to pan with bacon and cook until soft. Place beans, bacon, onion, chives and sage in a bowl. Add vinegar and oil to pan bacon was cooked in. Mix to remove cooking sediment.

3 Season with salt and pepper and pour over beans. Toss salad and serve.

Serves 4

Note: Green beans aren't my favourite vegetable. They are something to be suffered! Try them in this salad – they take on a whole new perspective.

Pickled Aubergine Salad

2 medium aubergines

salt

oil

4 cloves garlic

1 red pepper

1 cup chopped parsley

1 cup black olives

1 cup white vinegar

1 cup water

1 teaspoon salt

½ teaspoon fresh ground black pepper

¼ teaspoon cayenne pepper

1 Cut aubergine into 1cm slices. Sprinkle cut sides with salt and leave for 30 minutes. Wash salt from aubergine and dry slices on paper towels.

2 Heat oil in a frying pan and cook aubergine until lightly brown on each side. Drain on a paper towel. Crush and peel garlic. Cut into thin pieces. Deseed and slice pepper.

3 Layer aubergine, garlic, pepper, parsley and olives in a non-metallic dish. Heat vinegar, water, salt, freshly ground black pepper and cayenne pepper together until boiling. Remove from heat and pour over layered aubergine. Make sure all the aubergine is covered.

4 Cover dish and refrigerate for several hours before serving.

Serves 4

Note: This is a superb salad which is always enjoyed. It's a little fiddly but worth the effort.

Salad of Steamed Vegetables

12 baby carrots

250g asparagus

250g courgettes

100g mange tout

3 tomatoes

DRESSING

¼ cup olive oil

3 tablespoons red wine vinegar

1 tablespoon wholegrain mustard

freshly ground black pepper

1 Clean carrots and trim. Break ends from asparagus and trim spears to even lengths. Trim courgettes and cut into quarters lengthwise. Trim and string now peas.

2 Place prepared vegetables in a steamer and steam over boiling water for 10 to 15 minutes or until just tender. Refresh under cold running water. Drain.

3 Arrange on a platter. Chop tomato into 1cm cubes, discarding the core. Add to salad. Drizzle dressing over vegetables and leave for 1 hour before serving.

DRESSING

1 Place oil, vinegar, mustard and pepper in a screw top jar and shake until combined.

Serves 4

Beetroot Salad

2 medium beetroot

1 tablespoon sugar

½ cup chopped celery

½ cup roasted peanuts

½ cup chopped chives

½ cup vinaigrette

2 tablespoons sour cream

½ cup raspberry puree

1 Wash beetroot and peel. Grate beetroot into a bowl. Mix in sugar, celery, peanuts and chives. Mix vinaigrette, sour cream and raspberry puree together. Mix through beetroot mixture just before serving.

Serves 4

Note: Beetroot is such a hard vegetable to put anything with if you want it noticed, so go for flavour rather than looks for a successful beetroot salad. Use frozen or fresh raspberries.

potatoes

Garlic and Potato Mash

(see photograph on page 92)

1 kg large potatoes, cut into chunks

salt and black pepper

4 tablespoons olive oil

2 heads of garlic, cloves separated and peeled

1 red onion, chopped

3 tablespoons crème fraîche

4 tablespoons snipped fresh chives

1 Put the potatoes into a large saucepan of lightly salted boiling water, bring back to the boil, then simmer for 15–20 minutes, until tender.

2 Meanwhile, heat the oil in a heavy-based frying pan or saucepan over a low to medium heat. Add the garlic, cover the pan and cook gently for 10–15 minutes, until tender and golden at the edges. Remove the garlic and set aside. Add the onion to the oil and cook for 10 minutes or until softened.

3 Drain the potatoes, then return them to the pan and add the garlic, onion and oil. Mash well, stir in the crème fraîche and chives and season to taste.

Serves 4

Potato and Parsley Croquettes

(see photograph opposite)

90g long-grain rice

2 large potatoes, cut into chunks

2 red onions, finely chopped

1 clove garlic, crushed

4 tablespoons chopped fresh parsley

salt and black pepper

6 tablespoons sesame seeds

1 cup sunflower oil for frying

1 Cook the rice according to the packet instructions, until tender, then drain well. Spread it on a plate and leave for 1 hour or until completely cooled, fluffing it up with a fork occasionally.

2 Meanwhile, put the potatoes into a large saucepan of boiling salted water, then simmer for 15–20 minutes, until tender. Drain, then mash. Put the mashed potato into a large bowl with the cooled rice, onions, garlic, parsley and seasoning. Mix thoroughly.

3 Shape the mixture into 8 croquettes with your hands, then roll in the sesame seeds. Heat 1cm of oil in a large, heavy-based frying pan and fry the croquettes for 2–3 minutes, turning until crisp and browned all over.

Serves 4

Note: Crisp and golden outside and meltingly soft inside, these croquettes are very moreish. They're especially good served with a dollop of tangy tomato relish.

Potato and Olive Pie

melted butter

½ cup toasted breadcrumbs

4 cups mashed potato

¼ cup sundried tomato pesto

8 slices vegarian ham

1 cup pitted black olives

1 cup grated tasty cheese

¼ cup torn basil leaves

1 Grease a loose-bottom 20cm cake tin or springform tin liberally with melted butter. Place breadcrumbs in tin and toss to coat inside of tin.

2 Spread half the mashed potato over the base of the cake tin. Spread with pesto and lay prosciutto or ham over pesto. Top with a layer of olives. Spread remaining potato over the top. Sprinkle with grated cheese.

3 Bake at 200°C for 30 minutes or until heated through. Serve scattered with basil and cut into wedges to serve.

Serves 4–6

Potato and Apple Bake

4 medium onions

4 medium potatoes

4 medium apples

37g packet vegetable mix

2 cups water

½ teaspoon salt

1 tablespoon finely chopped fresh sage
 or 2 teaspoons dried sage

3 tablespoons butter

1 Peel onions and potatoes. Core apples with an apple corer. Cut onions, potatoes and apples into 0.5cm thick slices.

2 Place layers of onions, potato and apple into a 34 x 27cm casserole dish. Mix chicken soup with water. Add salt and pour over potato mixture. Sprinkle over sage and dot with butter.

3 Cover casserole with a lid or foil and bake at 200°C for 45 minutes. Remove lid and cook for a further 10 minutes.

Serves 6

Honey Roasted Spuds

6 medium potatoes

2 tablespoons oil

salt

½ cup liquid honey

chopped parsley or coriander

1 Peel potatoes. Cut into even-sized pieces. Cook in boiling salted water for 5 minutes or until tender on the outside but still uncooked on the inside. Drain and cool. Using a fork, run the tines of the fork over the outside of the potatoes.

2 Heat oil in a roasting dish or electric frying pan. Add potatoes and turn to coat. Sprinkle with salt.

3 Bake uncovered at 180°C for 30 minutes. Drizzle over honey. Continue to cook at 180°C for 25 to 30 minutes or until potatoes are tender. Sprinkle with parsley or coriander.

Serves 4

Note: These are deliciously different. Serve them with just about anything.

Potato Muffins

1½ cups plain flour

3 teaspoons baking powder

¼ teaspoon salt

60g butter

3 eggs

½ cup milk

2 cups grated potato

¼ cup chopped chives

1   Sift flour, baking powder and salt into a bowl. Make a well in the centre of the dry ingredients. Melt butter. Beat eggs and milk together. Pour butter and milk mixture into well with potato and chives. Mix quickly with a fork until ingredients are just combined.

2   Three-quarter fill greased muffin tins with mixture. Bake at 200°C for 10–15 minutes or until muffins spring back when lightly touched.

3   Serve hot as a main dish accompaniment.

Makes 12

Note: Try serving these instead of potatoes, rice or pasta

Italian Baked Potatoes

6 medium potatoes

400g can tomatoes in juice

2 cups grated mozzarella cheese

2 tablespoons chopped fresh basil or 1 tablespoon dried basil

½ cup grated Parmesan cheese

6 tablespoons olive oil

½ cup soft breadcrumbs

1 Peel the potatoes and cook in boiling salted water for 10 minutes. Drain well. Cool then cut into 1cm slices.

2 Arrange a layer of potatoes over the base of a greased, shallow, ovenproof dish. Pour over half the tomatoes and sprinkle with half the mozzarella cheese and one tablespoon of the basil. Sprinkle with half the Parmesan cheese. Pour over one tablespoon of the oil. Repeat the layers. Sprinkle with breadcrumbs and the remaining two tablespoons of oil.

3 Bake at 190°C for 30 minutes or until the potatoes are cooked and the top golden brown.

Serves 4–6

Tuscan Potatoes

6 medium potatoes

4 cloves garlic

¼ cup olive oil

1½ teaspoons dried rosemary

freshly ground black pepper

1 Peel potatoes and cut into 2cm cubes. Crush, peel and finely chop the garlic.

2 Heat the oil in a roasting pan. Add the potatoes, garlic and rosemary. Bake at 190°C for 30 to 40 minutes or until potatoes are cooked, turning potatoes frequently during cooking. Arrange on a serving plate and grind over black pepper.

Serves 4

Note: These potatoes are the sort of thing you develop a reputation on. They are simple, great tasting and put a modern slant on roast potatoes

Curried Potato and Egg Salad

6 medium potatoes

4 hard-boiled eggs

¼ cup chopped chives

2 sticks celery

½ cup mayonnaise

3 teaspoons curry powder

1 tablespoon finely chopped coriander

1   Peel potatoes. Cut into cubes and cook in boiling salted water until just tender. Drain well and place in a bowl. Shell the eggs and chop roughly. Add to the potatoes with the chives.

2   Wash and trim celery. Cut into thin slices. Add to the potatoes. Mix the mayonnaise and curry powder together and carefully mix through the potato mixture, taking care not to break up the potatoes. Garnish with chopped coriander.

Serves 4

Note: The amount of curry powder for this recipe will depend on your taste and the type of curry mix you use.

New Dimension Mashed Potato

6 medium potatoes

¼ cup potato cooking water

2 tablespoons butter

1 tablespoon grated lemon rind

freshly ground black pepper

1 Peel potatoes and cook in boiling salted water until tender. Drain, reserving ¼ cup of the cooking water. Mash potatoes and beat in cooking water, butter, lemon rind and pepper. Beat with a fork until smooth and creamy, adding a little milk if necessary. Serve immediately.

Serves 4–6

Note: Old potatoes make the best mashed potatoes. Banish the tomato sauce bottle from the table the day you serve these mashed potatoes.

Pesto Potatoes

6 medium potatoes

3 tablespoons prepared pesto

1 tomato

1 Peel potatoes. Cut into even-sized pieces and cook in boiling salted water for 15 to 20 minutes or until tender. Drain well. Place in a serving bowl. Drizzle over pesto. Cut tomato in half. Remove core and seeds. Cut flesh into strips. Pile on top of potatoes.

Serves 4–6

Note: Ready-made pesto is readily available from the chiller cabinet in the supermarket.

Sweet Potato and Honey Bake

4 medium sweet potatoes (or kumara)

2 tablespoons butter

2 teaspoons ground cumin

1 teaspoon ground coriander

432g can pineapple pieces in juice

about 1 cup vegetarian chicken stock

¼ cup honey

salt

freshly ground black pepper

chopped fresh coriander

1   Peel sweet potatoes and cut into 3cm pieces. Melt butter and mix in cumin and coriander. Drain pineapple, reserving juice.

2   Place sweet potato, butter mixture and pineapple in an ovenproof dish, preferably with a lid. Make pineapple juice up to 1½ cups with chicken stock. Mix in honey and pour over sweet potato. Season with salt and pepper.

3   Cover and cook at 180°C for 45 to 60 minutes until sweet potato is tender. Drain off excess liquid. Serve sprinkled with fresh coriander.

Serves 4

Note: Use frozen peeled sweet potato for this casserole if wished. They are much easier on your hands.

Sweet Potato Salad

3 medium sweet potatoes (or kumara)

4 spring onions

2 bananas

¼ cup lemon juice

½ cup low-fat sour cream

¼ cup mayonnaise

1 teaspoon curry powder

salt

freshly ground black pepper

1 tablespoon toasted sesame seeds

1   Peel sweet potatoes. Cut into pieces and steam or cook in boiling salted water for 15 minutes, or until tender. Drain and leave to cool. Slice spring onions on the diagonal into 1cm pieces. Peel bananas and cut in 0.5cm slices. Place in a bowl.

2   Pour lemon juice over bananas and mix to coat. When sweet potatoes are cold, cut into cubes. Mix sweet potato, spring onions and bananas together. Mix sour cream, mayonnaise, curry powder, salt and freshly ground black pepper together. Carefully mix through the sweet potato mixture. Place in a serving bowl and garnish with sesame seeds.

Serves 3–4

Note: This has appeared in my Salad and Barbecue books but it is so popular it is a must for a vegetable book. Add drained pineapple slices for a new slant on this delicious salad.

Potato Layer Bake

8 medium potatoes

1 clove garlic

¾ cup milk

¼ teaspoon grated nutmeg

salt

pepper

1 cup grated Gruyere cheese

1 Peel potatoes and slice thinly. Crush and peel garlic. Rub garlic over the bottom and sides of a greased, shallow casserole dish. Arrange potato slices in casserole dish. Mix milk and nutmeg together. Season with salt and pepper. Pour over potatoes. Top with grated cheese.

2 Cover and cook at 180°C for 40 to 45 minutes or until potatoes are tender. Remove lid and grill cheese until golden. Cut into wedges to serve.

Serves 6

Anon Potatoes

6 medium potatoes

2 tablespoons plain flour

1 egg

3 tablespoons milk

¼ cup vegetable oil

1 Peel potatoes, grate and drain in a sieve or colander, squeezing out as much liquid as possible. Lightly beat flour, egg and two tablespoons of milk together. Mix into grated potato. Add more milk if necessary to make a thin batter.

2 Heat oil in a frying pan and fry one-quarter cups full of mixture until golden on both sides. Serve immediately.

Serves 4–6

Note: Serve these as a vegetable accompaniment or as a light meal for a late weekend breakfast.

Italian Potato Salad

6 medium potatoes

4 rashers vegetarian bacon

1 cup black olives

½ cup drained pickled peppers

¼ cup fresh basil leaves

½ cup vinaigrette

1 Peel the potatoes and cut into thick slices. Cook in boiling salted water until tender. Drain well. Leave to cool. Cut vegetarian bacon into thin strips and cook for 3 to 5 minutes or until lightly browned.

2 Place the potatoes, olives, peppers, basil and bacon in a bowl. Carefully mix through the vinaigrette.

Serves 4–5

index

American Potato Salad	78		Fresh Vegetable Soup	29
Anon Potatoes	108		Fusilli with Aubergine and Tomatoes	54
Artichokes with Sour Cream Sauce	18		Garlic and Potato Mash	94
Asparagus and Tomato Salad with Cucumber	77		Green Bean Salad	88
Asparagus Polonaise	25		Green Beans and Mustard Sauce	34
Asparagus with Vinaigrette	24		Harvard Beets	41
Avocado Gazpacho	10		Honey Roasted Spuds	98
Baby Squash with Capsicum and Cheese Filling	22		Italian Baked Potatoes	100
Beetroot Salad	91		Italian aubergine Salad	75
Broccoli Soufflés with Olive Purée	22		Italian Potato Salad	109
Broccoli with Lemon Yoghurt Sauce	49		Italian Ribollita	27
Bruschetta and Crostini	10		Italian Spinach Tart	56
Brussels Sprouts with Almond Pesto	44		Leek, Lime and Coconut Soup	13
Brussels Sprouts with Horseradish	37		Lettuce, Avocado and Peanut Salad	72
Bulgar Wheat Salad with Grilled Peppers	83		Mixed-Mushroom and Goat's-Cheese Strudel	66
Caesar Salad	86		Mushroom and Black Olive Risotto	58
Celery Root and Herb Remoulade	36		Mushroom and Mange Tout Salad	76
Celery, Carrot and Apple Salad with Tahini	79		Mushroom Lasagne	68
Chilli Broccoli Spread	22		New Dimension Mashed Potato	103
Corn Cobs with Mixed Vegetables in Coconut Cream	35		Olla Gitana (Gypsy Stew)	43
Courgette and Hazelnut Salad	72		Oriental Coleslaw	82
Courgette and Mint Moulds with Fresh Tomato Sauce	44		Parsnip and Carrot Bake	39
Courgette Rounds with Pepper Purée	19		Pesto Potatoes	104
Creamy Aubergine Topping	14		Pickled Aubergine Salad	89
Curried Cream of Vegetable Soup	17		Potato and Apple Bake	97
Curried Potato and Egg Salad	102		Potato and Olive Pie	96
Deep-Fried Snake Beans	42		Potato and Parsley Croquettes	94
			Potato Layer Bake	107

Potato Muffins	99
Pumpkin and Pinenut Pasta Pie	66
Quick Calzone	60
Ratatouille	46
Red Cabbage with Apple and Walnuts	40
Roasted Pepper Salad	74
Roasted Pepper Topping	14
Roasted Vegetable and Broccoli Couscous	52
Roman Stuffed Tomatoes	55
Salad of Steamed Vegetables	90
Spicy Cauliflower and Potato	38
Spicy Wild-Rice Salad	80
Spinach and Almond Soup	14
Spinach and Ricotta Bake	26
Spinach and Roquefort Tart	59
Spinach Lasagne	60
Summer Tabbouleh	32
Sweet Pepper Terrine with Basil Vinaigrette	20
Sweet Potato and Honey Bake	105
Sweet Potato Salad	106
Sweet-and-Sour Red Cabbage	32
Thick Minestrone with Pesto	16
Three C's Carrot Soup	28
Tortilla with Corn and Sun-Dried Tomatoes	52
Tuscan Bean and Bread Soup	12
Tuscan Potatoes	101
Tuscan Vegetable Terrine	62
Vegetable Cannelloni	64

Vegetable Curry	48
Vietnamese Herbed Rice-Noodles with Peanuts and Asparagus	85
Walnut and Apple Coleslaw	86
Courgette and Hazelnut Salad	72
Courgette and Mint Moulds with Fresh Tomato Sauce	44
Courgette Rounds with Pepper Purée	19